Ju
Travel Guide

101 Places to Visit, Explore, and Experience Juneau, Alaska to the Fullest From A to Z

HowExpert with Caitlyn Knuth

For more tips related to this topic, visit www.HowExpert.com/travel.

Recommended Resources

www.HowExpert.com – Quick 'How To' Guides on Unique Topics by Everyday Experts.

www.HowExpert.com/writers- Write About Your #1 Passion/Knowledge/Experience.

www.HowExpert.com/membership - Learn a New 'How To' Topic About Practically Everything Every Week.

www.HowExpert.com/jobs - Check Out HowExpert Jobs.

Table of Contents

Chapter 1: Letting Go in Juneau

A Closer Look at the Last Frontier

Juneau, Alaska just may be one of the most dynamic cities the U.S. calls its own. From wild weather to inspiring wildlife, it's undeniably a city of extremes that feels like it's often a world away from the Lower 48. Alaska as a whole is considered the last true frontier and while Juneau finds its unique position in the rainforests and mountains of the Southeast, it comes with an equal measure of remote appeal. Juneau beckons travelers to come to take a look at something entirely different.

Considering this destination endures over 220 days of precipitation per year and no more than 85 days of recordable sunshine, it may be hard to imagine finding a sense of balance in a place of such incredible fluctuation...but it's possible. Travelers come to Juneau prepared for the bears only to be captivated by the peaceful, rolling fog. They arrive in the city expecting fishing boats and find themselves caught up in the sweet side of the local economy that can include chocolate and crepes. For many visitors, this sense of the unexpected is the most thrilling aspect of a visit to Juneau, Alaska. In the end, that's what frontier adventures are all about—getting out of your comfort zone and letting go in a space that's wild, free and wonderful in ways you didn't ever expect.

Capital City Connections

As the capital of Alaska, Juneau holds an important title for the state but is logistically unique from any other part of this sprawling land mass. Getting to Juneau is not as simple as jumping in the car and heading west. In fact, Juneau is the only capital city in the entire U.S. that cannot be accessed by land. Instead, visitors must be prepared to fly or sail their way into the capital city. While locals have mastered the art of the Alaska Marine Highway when they need to make their way to other destinations, the majority of visitors arrive by cruise ship during Juneau's peak visiting season that lasts from May through October. It is estimated that 1.3 million cruise ship passengers will visit Alaska in 2019 and with Juneau a major port of call for most cruise lines, this city of just over 32,000 year-round residents grows significantly during the summer months. While Juneau's population is considered average, its impressive land mass puts it on the map as the largest U.S. capital in terms of physical space.

A Few Things to Know Before You Go

Juneau is a city made for those with a heart for the great outdoors. While the downtown district brings a charming small-town feel with plenty of opportunities for shopping, it's hard to ignore the soaring mountains that frame Juneau's waterways. These peaks are impressively packed with dense rainforest which can be a surprise for those with visions of endless snowcaps dancing in their minds prior to arrival. From whales to eagles and the bears in between, Juneau promise to provide adventure on a scale that surpasses expectation. While the more experienced outdoor enthusiast may confidently head out into Juneau's bold terrain, it's highly recommended that first-time visitors take advantage of tour services in order to safely traverse this incredible landscape that above all belongs to nature itself.

Come to Juneau with the understanding that you'll encounter creatures of all kinds. Bald Eagles can often be spotted at the Port of Juneau if you happen to be arriving by cruise ship. They are frequently spotted on power lines and poles much like robins or crows might be observed in the Midwest. An afternoon salmon bake may lead to opportunities to see these fish fighting their way upstream at a nearby creek. Whale watching is abundant and the marine mammals you set off to see never fail to impress. Wherever you look, Juneau is a destination that reminds you that the balance between urban development and natural power is a delicate one at best.

Finally, a trip to Juneau requires a rain jacket, no matter when you arrive. While many destinations come with their fair share of over-dramatic warnings that can probably be disregarded to some extent, this is not one of them. Rain is common and rather constant in this region of Southeast Alaska and a sunny day can turn into an endless mist in moments. If you're prepared, it's hardly ever a problem and many soon come to find that there's something mystical and quite magical about this island city when the fog and rain roll in without warning.

The remote and thrilling nature of Juneau makes it a place perfect for travelers who are looking to make the most of dining, cultural excursions and the arts just as much as those who have their sights set on encounters of the wildlife kind. Whether you're here for the seafood, fascinated by the landscape or can't wait to get up close with a glacier, Juneau promises not to disappoint. There are many stories of visitors who arrived only to find leaving was too hard to fathom. Don't be surprised if somewhere in the middle of the fog, mist and fascinating scenery, you find you can't quite shake this one-of-a-kind destination when it's time to return home.

Chapter 2: Finding Your Way Through Flavor

Traveling to any destination across the planet is an experience in discovering new people, cultures, and traditions, but there's something special about finding your way through a new city with a flavorful twist that makes it truly unforgettable. Juneau is a city that comes to life for travelers in the summer months but no matter when you arrive in the capital, the one constant is an endless lineup of delicious dining options. Whether you're in the mood for something sweet, something exotic or something purely traditional, Juneau brings the savory variety in perfect balance. Come for the world-class salmon only to be captivated by the crepes. Come for the crab legs and find yourself falling in love with a small breakfast café that's hard to beat. Pick and choose or find time to try them all when you restaurant-hop your way through this gem of a destination in Southeast Alaska.

#1 Alaskan Crepe Escape

356 S. Franklin Street, Juneau, Alaska 99801

When you're craving something savory, there's no better eatery in Juneau to satisfy a sweet tooth quite like Alaskan Crepe Escape. Don't let the small size fool you, this French-inspired food stand serves up big flavor in style. Since it's opening in 2008, this creperie has been providing locals and visitors with the delights of French cuisine right in the heart of Alaska.

It's not a difficult locale to miss with the sign proudly boasting a rendition of the Eiffel Tower for all to enjoy. Guests can choose from options that include Sugar & Spice, Nutella and S'more flavored crepes as well as a collection of more robust lunch options including pizza, Greek and BBQ chicken flavors. A kid's menu keeps the little ones happy while those looking for a pick me up can indulge in handmade smoothies or a fresh cup of espresso upon request. Hang around and eat while making new friends or take your crepe to go and enjoy a beautiful day in Juneau with a fun side of flavor.

#2 Hangar on the Wharf

2 Marine Way #106, Juneau, Alaska 99801

For over 21-years Hangar on the Wharf has been a local hangout that hosts guests in the restored comforts of what was once a floatplane hangar. Today, this undeniable rustic-chic restaurant has earned the reputation as the establishment with the most extensive beer list in Juneau as well as a place that promises unsurpassed waterfront view and savory options you won't want to miss out on while you're here. While salads and wraps are plentiful, Hangar on the Wharf clearly has a way with seafood and it's hard to go wrong when you order the Halibut Chowder. From Wasabi Salmon Burgers to Alaskan Cod & Chips, those with a passion for prime seafood and a fun, laid-back setting won't be disappointed when they swing by Hangar on the Wharf.

For those that are interested in keeping tabs on the weather in Juneau for future hiking, fishing and exploring excursions, it's interesting to note that Hangar on the Wharf works closely with PTZtv as part of their webcam project and hosts a camera that captures the harbor and cruise ship terminal 24-hours a day. Hangar on the Wharf provides a perfect vantage point to see the cruise ships arrive and depart and gives those looking to get out on the water a better idea of conditions for the day as well.

#3 The Alaskan Fudge Co.

313 Carrol Way, Juneau, Alaska 99801

The Alaskan Fudge Company has been a household name in Juneau since this family-run business first opened in 1980. Hosting an impressive and seemingly endless lineup of truffles, fudge, chocolate turtles and beyond, passer-by's shouldn't be surprised when they're drawn through the front doors by the decadent aroma that lingers around this establishment. Purchase your favorite chocolates and fudge by the pound or by the box. While The Alaskan Fudge Company is a great stop for a sweet treat, it proves just as successful at providing visitors with the perfect souvenir by which to remember their Juneau adventures. If you happen to be traveling to Juneau with young children, The Alaska Fudge Co. is also home to some fluffy and friendly plush pals that make it easy for little ones to cozy up to a new best friend during their travels through Southeast Alaska.

#4 Tracy's King Crab Shack

432 S. Franklin Street, Juneau, Alaska 99801

While those hailing from the lower 48 may find crab legs and bisque to be a delicious delicacy, the waters surrounding Juneau are teeming with mouth-watering potential and there's no place better to savor the flavor than Tracy's King Crab Shack. While this well-loved waterfront establishment serves up other seafood bites, its reputation has long been built on its crab leg offerings. Crab cakes, Jasmine Rice and a variety of daily specials make Tracy's memorable but it's the crab leg combos that keep locals and visitors coming back for more. Whether you're in the mood for a single leg or an entire bucket of flavor, Tracy's King Crab Shack has 12-years of experience serving up Juneau's finest crab-based fare.

#5 Imperial Saloon

241 Front Street, Juneau, Alaska 99801

When you're looking for a place to relax, unwind and enjoy a drink like a local, make your way to Imperial Saloon and be a part of Juneau's beverage-based history. As the oldest bar in the city, Imperial Saloon holds a special place in the hearts of Juneau residents and continues to provide first class service since its establishment in 1891. Feel free to order up something cold and savory before settling in at the long bar or picking a comfortable place at one of Imperial Saloon's many traditional tables. The atmosphere is laid-back and the point of it all is clearly to have fun. Both a pool table and ping pong table are waiting to help guests pass an enjoyable afternoon or evening with some friendly competition.

#6 The Narrows

148 S. Franklin Street, Juneau, Alaska 99801

If you're all dressed up with nowhere to go, The Narrows has you covered. This small and elegant establishment specializes in craft cocktails and spirits. Located downtown, The Narrows is a popular place to grab a drink before heading out for a night on the town or simply passing a great evening with friends. Try everything from a Long Island Iced Tea to a decadent Martini garnished to perfection as you enjoy the fun that comes with a glamorous locale and the company of good friends. Have a special request? The staff at The Narrows is known for their warm welcome and creative spirit and it's likely that they can bring your beverage ideas to life right in front of your eyes if you ask.

#7 Zerelda's Bistro

9351 Glacier Highway, Juneau, Alaska 99801

Loved by locals for its friendly atmosphere and incredibly flavorful dishes, Zerelda's Bistro is owned by Juneau local Abby LaForce who brought this culinary establishment to life in 2016, naming it after her grandmother whose influence instilled a love of cooking from the start. Today, guests visit Zerelda's to enjoy everything from a cup of coffee and a pastry to small snack plates or a savory dinner. Additionally, there's something wonderful about knowing you're dining in an establishment that's built on local memory and skills that have been passed down through generations. Dinner reservations are highly recommended for those looking to end their night on a delicious note at Zerelda's Bistro with options that include everything from seared scallops to Moroccan braised lamb.

#8 Deckhand Dave's

139 S. Franklin Street, Juneau, Alaska 99801

The city of Juneau is largely defined by its vast fishing culture, so it makes sense that marine life has cultivated much of the culinary scene as well. Perhaps no place in the city captures the spirit of living off the sea's many marine gifts quite like Deckhand Dave's. This specialty taco truck highlights combinations of seafood all wrapped in a savory tortilla made to taste. A casual atmosphere, friendly staff and focus on fine seafood makes this one of Juneau's best places to stop and grab a bite whenever a craving hits. There's no need to rush when you choose to have lunch at Deckhand Dave's. This culinary hot spot is popular with locals and visitors and is a great place to grab a bite and maybe meet some new people while you're at it.

#9 Twisted Fish Company Alaskan Grill

550 S. Franklin Street, Juneau, Alaska 99801

Seafood is a Juneau dining option favorite, but when it comes to pairing your fish with the perfect wine selection, nobody does it better than the staff at Twisted Fish Company Alaskan Grill. This rustic and elegant establishment maintains a laid-back atmosphere that displays natural wood beam walls and plays host to a gorgeous floor to ceiling stone fireplace. Its downtown location makes it a popular waterfront hangout for locals and visitors alike looking for something savory to enjoy with a white, red or rosé selection in hand. Feel free to come in for a small plate of fresh oysters or stick around and indulge in entrees that include everything from Alaskan King Crab legs to Black Cod Picatta. If you're not sure what drink to match your meal selection, the staff is well-versed in pairings and is happy to provide advice on where to start and end your savory journey.

#10 Sandpiper Café

429 W. Willoughby Avenue, Juneau, Alaska 99801

Juneau is packed with potential when it comes to restaurants made for a delightful dinner. When it comes to breakfast and brunch options, Sandpiper Café steps up as the ideal stop in the capital city.

While vegetarian and vegan menu options make this a versatile dining stop for those who abide by dietary restrictions, those who swing by with kids in tow will appreciate the variety of breakfast food options that are sure to please. Open from 6 am until 2 pm daily, the Sandpiper Café is the place to be when you're craving everything from hash to scrambles and maybe even a burger in between. This destination is also well-loved for its friendly staff and overall welcoming atmosphere no matter when you arrive.

#11 Pier 49

406 S. Franklin Street #102, Juneau, Alaska 99801

When you're looking to cure a craving while indulging in the best waterfront view in town, Pier 49 checks every box. Open-air seating with water below and mountains ahead provides the perfect backdrop when you're looking forward to enjoying a decadent seafood dish. A full-service bar complete with handcrafted cocktail options means the perfect beverage pairing for your savory meal is never far from reach. Enjoy the added charm of twinkling bistro lights overhead making this a dining destination in Juneau you won't soon forget.

#12 The Rookery Café

111 Seward Street, Juneau, Alaska 99801

Juneau is a versatile destination when it comes to landscape, culture, and history, so it should come as no surprise that the food scene is no exception to the rule. For those visitors looking for a place that provides a dynamic selection of eclectic burgers as well as plates that highlight Asian-infusion, The Rookery Café will have your taste buds tingling. This unique culinary destination is worth stopping in when you're looking for a great cup of coffee or hoping to dine on meticulously garnished seared scallops. The combination of chalkboard menus, vibrant art, and friendly staff keep The Rookery Café a one-of-a-kind Juneau locale that shouldn't be missed. Come in for the unique sense of style this café offers up, and you'll end up staying in great part thanks to the welcoming staff and incredible menu options.

#13 Red Dog Saloon

278 S. Franklin Street, Juneau, Alaska 99801

Channeling the charm of the wild west, Red Dog Saloon invites hungry guests to make their way through the swinging front doors and step into a world away from the rainforest covered mountains of Southeast Alaska. Sawdust covers the floor while delicious dishes cover the tables in this fun, themed restaurant that inevitably has guests lingering well beyond the end of their meal. Costumed staff serve up everything from burgers to ribs and with plenty of beer on tap, there's no reason not to make an afternoon or evening of it when you stop by Red Dog Saloon.

#14 The Alaskan Brewing Company

5364 Commercial Boulevard, Juneau, Alaska 99801

Since its founding in 1986, The Alaskan Brewing Company has made a strong name for itself on the brew scene in Juneau. Their award-winning labels are frequent contestants in international brew competitions and continue to delight Alaskans as well as those in the lower 48 with bold flavors and smooth style. As these fantastic flavors of the Last Frontier continue to gain popularity, The Alaskan Brewing Company finds it influences reaching into a 23rd state in 2019. Those interested in taking up the art of brewing may find it interesting that The Alaskan Brewing Company frequently posts adds for Brew Masters and Operators at their Juneau headquarters. Travelers looking to switch things up for a season or maybe even permanently on the professional front will want to take time to talk to the staff about these intriguing on-site opportunities when they stop in.

Chapter 3: Making the Most of Amazing Views

Travelers looking for a destination that combines the best of sea, land, and sky don't have to look far to find it all in Juneau, Alaska. While the city's accessibility by water makes it a popular destination for cruise ship passengers, those with a heart for the great outdoors are drawn to Juneau by sky in search of spectacular vistas that are unlike any other on the map. A single visit to this dynamic destination brings you within reach of fjords, gorgeous glaciers, towering mountain peaks and thick emerald rainforests that crawl up impossibly steep cliffsides. Combined with the mist and fog that roll in on a moment's notice, there's a reason Juneau is often fondly remembered by travelers who have returned home with a sense of mystique. If the terrain isn't enough to take your breath away, the wildlife surely will be. A diverse landscape lends itself to being the ideal ecosystem for bears, eagles, salmon, whales and many more. Make the most of your time in Alaska's capital by making a plan to maximize exposure to amazing views. While they seem to be everywhere, the best are often found with just a bit of work and the enthusiasm to pursue off-the-beaten-path adventure.

#15 Downtown Harbor

510 S. Franklin Street, Juneau, Alaska 99801

The majority of tourists who make their way to Juneau will arrive by cruise ship, making downtown Juneau Harbor an inevitable and wonderful stop on the journey through the state capital. Most will agree this is for the best as the downtown harbor provides some of the most stunning views around. Before heading off to pre-planned excursions, take time to soak up the scenery that's comprised of steeply forested mountains, soaring eagles overhead, waterways dotted with wooden docks and boats bobbing in nearby marinas. Locals frequent the harbor in the name of business, but it also provides the perfect excuse to simply wander for wandering sake. Don't forget to appreciate the spectacular view that comes with the arrival and departure of cruise ships in this area too. If you're hopping off a cruise ship to explore, the view from below is sure to be a welcome sight. For those visiting Juneau and arriving by air, it can be a breathtaking moment to witness these massive ships come into port or make their way out towards distance destinations.

#16 Auke Bay Harbor

Coordinates: 58.377469, -134.725428

Once you've had time to experience downtown's famous harbor, make your way north for a chance to indulge in the beauty of Auke Bay Harbor as well. Meticulously maintained pathways line Auke Bay, making the harbor a beautiful place to come and spend an afternoon walking and admiring the many fishing boats that make their way through the glittering waters. While enchanting superyachts are sometimes moored in this area, it's more common to see a variety of whale-watching vessels leaving from Auke Bay Harbor in pursuit of some truly spectacular marine sights further out. Tranquil and endlessly intriguing, Auke Bay Harbor is a good solution for those looking to escape the hustle and bustle of downtown activities while still remaining in a populated area close to the scenic beauty.

#17 Mount Roberts Tramway

490 S. Franklin Street, Juneau, Alaska 99801

If you arrive in Juneau by cruise ship, the Mount Roberts Tramway is nearly impossible to miss. Towering into the sky on a backdrop of emerald forest, mountain and sea, this aerial tramway first opened in 1996 and continues to thrill visitors to this day. While the ascent is only 6-minutes total, the view lasts a lifetime. As you rise 1,800 feet into the air, an impressive and dynamic landscape quickly comes into view. At the top, enjoy sweeping vistas from the Mountain House which highlight the stunning combination of Juneau and the Gastineau Channel. An all-day pass for the tramway can be purchased for just $35 when a single ride just won't be enough to satisfy. While the Mount Roberts Tramway is a necessary mode of transportation for those looking to reach new heights in Juneau, it's also a fun way to spend some time for those travelers looking for a quick and sure adrenaline rush upon arrival to the city.

#18 Shrine of St. Therese

21425 Glacier Highway, Juneau, Alaska 99801

St. Therese of Lisieux holds the title as the patron saint of Juneau, making a trip to the Shrine of St. Therese a beautiful and meaningful experience for locals and visitors alike in the city. Situated 22-miles north of downtown, this shrine isn't far from the primary drop off points for cruise ship passengers, but like many landmarks in Juneau, one must navigate through nature in order to find it. Tucked into the Tongass National Forest, the shrine is a combination of stone and gold, creating a gorgeous work of architecture where visitors can honor the importance of love and dedication to something greater than one's self. Visitors come to pray and meditate within the tranquility provided by the forest and water while others come to admire the chapel. However you spend your time, the Shrine of St. Therese is by far one of the most scenic stops Juneau freely offers up.

#19 Silverbow Basin

Coordinates: 58.3100 N, 134.3444 W

If you're up for a hike in the name of encountering some of Juneau's most beautiful hidden treasures, a trek to Silverbow Basin is meant for you. This dynamic valley situated on Gold Creek Sits just over 2-miles northeast of the City Center and is much appreciated for its mountainous landscape. Beyond its alluring façade, Silverbow Basin intrigues travelers with it' history steeped in gold. In fact, this very valley is often credited with being the location where Joe Juneau first discovered gold in Southeast Alaska. Eventually, this discovery would lead to the founding and naming of the city of Juneau itself.

Chapter 4: Guided Tours and Excursions

Travelers with an insatiable sense for adventure will be tempted to take on Juneau solo. Intrigued by the mountains, water and forest it's easy to find oneself ready to set off for the experience of a lifetime into the great unknown without truly being prepared for the excitement or potential for problems along the way. While locals and those who frequent Juneau may find the many routes to adventure more manageable with time, it's highly recommended that first-time visitors or those who are less acquainted with the great outdoors take full advantage of the plethora of tour and excursions opportunities Juneau has to offer. There are a wide variety of company options when it comes to maximizing time touring Juneau. Whether you're in the mood for whale watching, participating in a salmon bake, looking to get up and hike a glacier or hoping for a bird's eye view from a helicopter, there's no shortage of organizations and companies willing to help out. Here are just a few of the many available to travelers who arrive and can't wait to see what's out there while keeping safety top of mind.

#20 Whale Watching-Alaska Travel Adventures

9085 Glacier Highway #301, Juneau, Alaska 99801

As one of Juneau's longest-running tour organizations, Alaska Travel Adventures is a wonderful company to work with when organizing whale watching excursions in Juneau. The waters that surround the capital are home to a variety of extraordinary marine mammals including humpbacks, orcas, and dolphins, making whale watching not only thrilling but practically guaranteed during the summer season. Booking a whale watching excursion with Alaska Travel Adventures is an approximately 3.5-hour event that comes complete with transportation to the pier from the meeting point under Mount Roberts Tramway.

A knowledgeable onboard naturalist meets you at the water and is there to guide you onto your whale watching vessel. These whale watching boats come complete with extra-large windows, an outdoor viewing deck, and are propeller-free. This means you'll have the opportunity to see these incredible creatures in action while protecting whales and surrounding marine mammals from potential harm. Throughout the course of your whale watching excursion, your onboard guide and naturalist is there to narrate the adventure with helpful information related to the surrounding scenery and the migratory whale pods that call Juneau home for several months out of the year. Feel free to ask questions as they come up because your guide is ready to provide answers and help you identify whales by their many specific markings and behaviors too!

#21 Salmon Bake-Alaska Travel Adventures

1061 Salmon Creek Lane, Juneau, Alaska 99801

Since 1978, Alaska Travel Adventures has taken the flavor, fun, and thrill of Alaskan adventures and combined them into unforgettable package deal experiences for guests. While it's often paired with a whale watching excursion, the salmon bake at Gold Creek is a savory stop that keeps guests coming back for more. Once you're dropped off at the site with the help of a bright yellow salmon bake bus that's hard to miss, the options are delicious and endless. Enjoy a vast all-you-can-eat buffet that includes everything from Tongass wild rice and cornbread to hot chowder and baked beans. Of course, the highlight of the meal is the wild Alaska salmon expertly cooked up on an outdoor Alderwood grill. Be sure to ask for the brown sugar topping for an added sweetness to what is bound to be an amazing meal.

As an added bonus, guests to the Gold Creek salmon bake will be entertained with live, acoustic music as musicians play a soundtrack of songs that perfectly fit the mood and feel of exploring Southeast Alaska for the very first time. An on-site gift shop makes it easy to pick up that perfect souvenir before you head on your way. However, for those that are looking for a bit more outdoor adventure, the Gold Creek salmon bake site links up with a short trail allowing guests to view salmon swimming upstream and ending with a series of waterfalls that make for an amazing picture.

#22 Mendenhall Glacier Hike-Liquid Alaska Tours

6000 Glacier Spur Road, Juneau, Alaska 99801

Juneau is a land of gorgeous glaciers and while they are receding at an alarming rate, tour companies are becoming more adept at finding routes to providing visitors with opportunities to see these natural wonders in a way that's safe for people and nature. Booking a Mendenhall Glacier hike with Liquid Alaska Tours provides a 5.5-hour experience on this massively impressive ice river that runs half a mile wide and nearly 2,000 feet deep. Equipment and safety gear are provided in the cost of the journey. Be prepared to be thrilled by the fact you'll have the chance to leave a footprint on waves of traveling ice before they retreat into the pages of history.

#23 Dog Sledding Experience-Alaska Shore Excursions

212 Admiral Way #5, Juneau, Alaska 99801

Dog sledding is an activity that is tightly woven into Alaskan culture. Whether it's for recreation or necessity when it comes to moving food and materials across vast landscapes, the art of mushing and the Huskies that pull the sled are an integral part of many Alaskan's lives. Guests have the chance to get the feel for this thrilling sport by booking a dog sledding tour with Alaska Shore Excursions during their visit. This tour is often combined with a helicopter tour that takes guests up to Herbert glacier where one of Juneau's most notorious dog sledding kennels is located. Guests take a kennel tour to understand what it takes to care for the amazing dogs that make dog sledding possible. If you happen to come at just the right time of year, be prepared to encounter some serious charm as puppies make their grand debut on-site. After the tour, enjoy a dog sled experience for yourself as you glide over thrilling terrain. Before you head out, tour guides will instruct visitors in the language and commands that have long been used by professional mushers.

#24 Douglas Island Zipline Tour-Alaska Canopy Adventures

76 Eagan Drive #100, Juneau, Alaska 99801

Just across the bridge from Juneau lies Douglas Island, known and loved for its scenic beauty, delightful downtown scene, and undeniably mountainous terrain. This combination makes it the perfect destination for taking in Juneau and Douglas Island from high above the ground. Booking a zipline tour with Alaska Canopy Adventures is a wonderful way to speak to a passion for adrenaline-pumping thrills while earning a once in a lifetime view of this incredible landscape. Guests on this tour have the opportunity to enjoy a total of five ziplines, as well as a suspension bridge that brings the vast and dynamic landscape of Southeast Alaska to life within moments of pushing off the platform. With one of the ziplines on this tour measuring 600-feet in length, this is an experience that's built for the great adventurer and definitely not for the faint of heart or heights.

#25 Alaska Boat and Kayak

11521 Glacier Highway, Juneau, Alaska 99801

If you're a traveler who prefers to take to the waterways independently, be sure to put Alaska Boat and Kayak at the top of your must-visit list. Since opening in 1996, this store has been offering unsurpassed water safety and skills classes as well as renting top-quality equipment and gear that lets guests get out and enjoy a safe and incredible experience around the waters of Juneau. While they offer plenty of guided tours upon request, rental services extend to kayaks and stand up paddleboards depending on what type of water-based adventure you're looking for. Even if you're an experienced outdoor explorer, Alaska Boat and Kayak is the place to ask questions or get a quick refresher on techniques and best practices. The staff at this locale is happy to offer up helpful advice no matter how many times you've been out on the water before.

#26 Above and Beyond Alaska

2767 Sherwood Lane, Juneau, Alaska 99801

For those visitors to Juneau who appreciate a small-group approach to touring, Above and Beyond Alaska provides a more intimate feel to experiences that include whale watching, glacier hiking and much more. From customized tours that focus on Alaskan specialty gourmet meals to those that take small groups to those place that are likely to provide encounters with black bears, Above and Beyond Alaska makes it easy and comfortable to approach the incredible terrain Juneau provides. This company also brings a focus on environmental protection and conservation throughout their tour offerings, making it a great choice for those who are looking to go-green when they go touring.

#27 Icefield Helicopter Tour-Coastal Helicopters

8995 Yandukin Drive, Juneau, Alaska 99801

Juneau brings some jaw-dropping scenery from a ground-based perspective, so imagine what it could be like to get above the clouds and take it all in from a bird's eye view. That's exactly what Coastal Helicopters provides to those guests to Juneau that book an Icefield Helicopter tour. Icefields, ponds, glaciers, endless crevasses and towering mountain sides are all yours for the enjoying when you include this tour on your Juneau itinerary. Leaving from the Juneau International Airport, guests will hop onboard a helicopter piloted by an experienced and certified professional ready to narrate your amazing trip from the moment you take off to the moment you land once more. While most of the experience is spent in the air, guests are invited to take a stroll on Herbert Glacier when you come in for a brief yet breathtaking landing.

#28 Alaskan Fishing Experience-Moore Charters, LLC

11957 Glacier Highway, Juneau, Alaska 99801

While Moore Charters, LLC offers whale watching experiences for those looking to observe underwater wonders, visiting anglers quickly fall in love with this company for its salmon and halibut chartered fishing experiences. You don't have to be an expert to make the most of your chartered experience on the waters surrounding Juneau. Accompanied by an experienced and certified captain, you'll have time to take in plenty of tips, tricks, and advice before heading out on the water to see just what you can catch. All of the equipment you'll need is provided onboard, all you need to do is show up and be willing to give it a try. This is a great option for an experienced angler as well as the accompanying captain is a great resource for added knowledge or a simple refresher on some well-loved strategies on the water.

Chapter 5: Natural Wonders

To step back and view the city of Juneau, Alaska from a distance is to feel as if you're witnessing a storybook come to life. Without the hustle and bustle of the city's population in your ears, Juneau's profile is one dominated by towering mountains, glittering waters and a blanket of fog that comes and goes as it pleases. In a place where stark white mountain goats can be spotted lingering on mountainsides covered in lush green forest, it's hard to imagine a more pristine place on earth.

An up-close look at it all is even better. Juneau is a city built for fun, entertainment and flavor but at its core, it is a city that thrives within the greater context of the many natural wonders that call this destination home. With the Tongass National Forest delivering up a thriving ecosystem of potential, guests to Juneau are thrilled to find that within the woods, a glacier appears. Blue ice dots a landscape otherwise saturated with waterfalls, snow-capped mountain peaks and unassuming beaches that are regularly frequented by spectacular sea lions. No matter where you go, Juneau holds a mystery in the form of natural landmarks. While you're here, be sure to find the time to hit the highlights and don't forget your camera while you do.

#29 Mendenhall Glacier

6000 Glacier Spur Road, Juneau, Alaska 99801

As one of the most impressive glaciers in Juneau, it's not surprising that Mendenhall Glacier is also the most visited of them all in this area. Sitting in the depths of Tongass National Forest, Mendenhall Glacier is most accessible by the Visitor Center which provides a starting point from which to hike and view this amazing phenomenon of icy nature. Guests are endlessly thrilled by the vast trail of blue and white ice that spans 13-miles and ends with a steep drop off and often crash in Mendenhall Lake. Only a small number of permits are issued to climb or hike the glacier on an annual basis so those who have come to make the most of the moment from a distance won't want to forget their camera. Plenty of viewing areas are available near the glacier and if you're willing to make the hike up the trail from the Visitor Center, you're sure to be glad you did.

#30 Mt. Juneau

Travel Juneau 800 Glacier Avenue #201, Juneau, Alaska 99801

The many peaks that call Juneau home are sure to impress but standing out from them all, Mt. Juneau brings something special and significant to the landscape. At an elevation of 3,576-feet, Mt. Juneau is a dramatic mountain that never fails to mesmerize even the most experienced of mountain enthusiasts and climbers. Providing a gorgeous mix of alpine and coastal forest, Mt. Juneau is an outdoor lover's dream. It's a mountain that's best suited to experienced climbers as it's considered steep and rugged most of the way up and the terrain can be decidedly unexpected. It should also be noted that Mt. Juneau comes with a hefty set of avalanche warnings, making it a place where pristine beauty and a significant amount of danger exist.

#31 Nugget Falls

Coordinates: 58.4272 N, 134.5367 W

The combination of rainforest, mountains, glaciers, and waterways means that cascade chasers are never short on options to view amazing waterfalls when they're in Juneau. While there are plenty to choose from, Nugget Falls tops the list when it comes to impressive displays of natural power. Nugget Falls is accessible by using the East Glacier Loop and requires nothing more than a 15-minute walk to reach the cascade. As water rushes from a height of over 300-feet in the air, the beauty of the experience is amplified by the fact the waterfall is framed by the blue ice of the nearby glacier and emerald foliage above. Impressive and inspiring, Nugget Falls is the perfect photo opportunity for those looking to capture the essence of Juneau on camera.

#32 Tongass National Forest

28955 Glacier Highway, Juneau, Alaska 99801

While Juneau may give off the impression of being small-town in ambiance, its nature says otherwise. Tongass National Forest is, in fact, the largest of all that exist in the United States. Covering the majority of Southeast Alaska, Tongass National Forest spans over 16 million acres of land and is home to some of Juneau's most incredible natural landmarks including Mendenhall Glacier. It's the ideal place to catch a glimpse of bears hunting fish, eagles soaring through the skies or salmon making their way upstream during spawning season. While there's a lot to explore, taking time to experience even a small portion of this amazing place is worth your time.

#33 Jensen-Olsen Arboretum

23035 Glacier Highway, Juneau, Alaska 99801

The natural beauty that Juneau offers up is undeniable, but what might be even more impressive is the efforts put into finding a way to tame aspects of nature into designs that are made to inspire. The Jensen-Olsen Arboretum on Pearl Harbor was gifted to the city by Caroline Jensen who was a lifelong master gardener. Beds of breathtaking floral color make up the vast majority of this arboretum and are designed to frame the natural beauty of the mountains, forests, and water that lies just beyond its borders. It's a destination that speaks to those with a passion for horticulture as well as visitors looking for a new and dynamic level of landscaping that provides the perfect balance between human effort and mother nature's best, unaided work.

#34 Eagle Beach

28955 Glacier Highway, Juneau, Alaska 99801

Those visitors looking to indulge in some truly unbelievable landscapes will want to make time for a trip to Eagle Beach during their stay in Juneau. As a designated State Recreation Site, Eagle Beach is highly-valued and protected land that continues to be a place bears, eagles, fish, and whales call home. From the beach, visitors can take in unobstructed views of Lynn Canal and the Chilkat Mountains. Eagle Beach is a popular destination for campers but also provides several river bars ideal for those looking to spend some tranquil time fishing. Be sure to keep your eyes open for sea lions that are commonly viewed in this area.

#35 Tracy Arm Fjord

Allen Marine Tours-13391 Glacier Highway, Juneau, Alaska 99801

Sitting 45-minutes south of central Juneau, those looking to experience the beauty of Tracy Arm Fjord will need to organize water transportation or a day tour to make the most of this incredible sight. It's more difficult to reach location means Tracy Arm Fjord enjoys less traffic than Mendenhall Glacier and just as spectacular of views. A combination of blue and white ice provides a stark contrast against the 3,000-foot cliffs that rise up to frame this natural wonder. The cliffs are dotted with small cascades adding to the dramatic overall effect of the visit. While it's positioned in a rather small inlet, Tracy Arm Fjord is nothing short of vast and impressive.

#36 Granite Creek

Coordinates: 58.314403, - 134.35021

As notorious as the trail that bears its same name, Granite Creek is a must-see natural wonder for those who are interested in close encounters with impressive terrain and endless cascades. The creek weaves through breathtaking granite walls that are sprinkled with waterfalls along the way. While many hikers seek out Granite Creek for the challenging trek it provides, visitors looking for the perfect photo opportunity don't have to look far when they visit this well-loved destination in Juneau.

Chapter 6: Wildlife Encounters

It's easy to get caught up in the breathtaking beauty of Juneau to the point of sometimes forgetting that it is first and foremost home to an impressive number of exotic, powerful and fascinating wildlife. Not to fear, the forgetting doesn't last long as inevitably, along your way, you'll encounter an animal that reminds you just how amazing of a place the shores of Southeast Alaska can be. When it comes to bears, Alaska is full of them, however, Juneau and the rest of the Southeastern portion of the state are particularly desirable for these animals as the seafood is plentiful and the wilderness is vast. The city of Juneau has worked hard to create and maintain spaces throughout the city and beyond that make it possible to view bears in their natural habitats while maintaining a safe distance. That being said, the bears care little for human policies and it's not unheard of to see a bear make its way near or through downtown on occasion.

While bears are an icon of Juneau's wildlife status, the city also plays host to an amazing number of eagles, mountain goats, whales, orcas, seals as well. Bald eagles will often perform impressive aerial displays as guests to the city disembark from a cruise ship and can swiftly be spotted near popular destinations such as the Mount Roberts Aerial Tramway. Agile mountain goats may require a spotting scope, but whales and orcas are more easily spotted by booking a spot on a certified tour. Be sure to make plans to see these inspiring creatures while you're here, but more importantly, be prepared to be pleasantly surprised when they show up on their own.

#37 Bear Spotting at Steep Creek Trail

Coordinates: 58.417617, -134.565979

While the thought of running unexpectedly into one of nature's most powerful creatures is a cause for hesitation, bears are an integral part of Juneau's natural landscape. Picking out a safe observation point is key for those that are looking to maintain high standards of safety for both themselves and the creatures they are there to observe. The Steep Creek Trail runs near the Mendenhall Glacier Visitor Center and a bear viewing platform has been established to make it simple and safe for visitors to watch the many bears that amble through in search of salmon. While the platform is connected to fenced walkways perfect for observation, it's important for visitors to remember to use caution and common sense around these wild creatures that call Juneau home.

#38 Salmon Run at Amalga Harbor

Coordinates: 58.4947 N, 134.7933 W

There's something incredible about witnessing a salmon run and there's no better place to do it than Amalga Harbor. While this scenic destination was enough to inspire Ernest Gruening to write a manifesto in 1953 on why Alaska should be a state, it continues to inspire visitors as a prime place to view wildlife in action. At high tide, salmon find their way through a narrow creek mouth in astonishing numbers. While they aren't an option for fishing at this point in their run, they're incredible strength and perseverance is amazing none the less. Orcas and sea lions are highly in tune with the changing tides and arrival of so many salmon, so don't be surprised if you have company during your viewing.

#39 Eagle Spotting at Gastineau Channel

Coordinates: 58.295 N, -134.4072222 W

The Bald Eagle is a fierce and fascinating bird of prey that is commonly spotted in Juneau, much to the delight of visitors. Anywhere along the Gastineau Channel, eagles can be viewed soaring mountainside or perched in the lush foliage above. With wingspans that can reach up to 7-feet in length and stark white feathers on their heads, these avian raptors are an incredible sight to behold.

#40 Sea Lions at Eagle Beach

Coordinates: 58.5292 N, 134.8286 W

Sea lions may not first spring to mind when you're considering a trip to Juneau, but they call this area home in impressive numbers and can make for a truly spectacular surprise. Make your way to Eagle Beach during the summer months for the best chance at seeing these agile and often vocal creatures spending time in their natural habitat. The waters around Eagle Beach are often teeming with fish, making this a prime viewing area for those sea lions on the hunt for something savory after an extended nap on the rocky shores.

#41 Whale Watching at Glacier Bay

Coordinates: 58.6658 N, 136.9002 W

A day tour through Glacier Bay is a wonderful way to spend time in search of amazing humpback whales and orcas that dominate the waters around Juneau and up through the Inside Passage. The waters near Bartlett Cove tend to be a hot spot for marine mammal activity and those who are booked on tours to explore this area alongside a knowledgeable guide will likely find themselves lingering in these waters for a chance to get an up-close look at the majesty of these underwater wonders. There are a limited number of tour operators that make these journeys with guests for good reason.

While Glacier Bay National Park and Preserve spans a breathtaking 3.3-million acres of combined water and land, it's one of the most pristine and protected areas on the planet. With this prestigious title comes a number of boating restrictions put in place to maintain the integrity of Glacier Bay for future generations. Private boaters looking to visit Glacier Bay must apply for a permit within 60 days of a planned excursion and once the permit is secured, it is only valid for seven days. Permits are only available on a first come first serve basis between June and early August. Experienced private boat owners know the value of such a permit and are quick to secure one as they go extremely quickly. Travelers to the area that are looking for extended trips to Glacier Bay National Park and Preserve will want to be aware of the fact that the only tour companies that operate this type of excursion depart from Gustavus.

Chapter 7: Hiking Trails and Camping Hot Spots

Hiking in and around Juneau is a favorite pastime for most locals and those who move to Juneau from out of town quickly pick up a habit for hitting the trails and making the most of the great outdoors. Whether you're looking for a challenging trek that pushes the limits of human athleticism, seeking a trail that comes with drastic changes in elevation or a short and sweet jaunt through the woods, there's a little something for everyone when it comes to hiking. When you're looking for the perfect place to set up camp and call it a night, there's ample space, wilderness and wild for that as well. Many campsites in Juneau come equipped to welcome a range of tents and RV's meaning it's simple to create the experience you're craving.

The benefit of hiking and camping in and around Juneau is closely linked to the amazing terrain that covers the island. You don't have to hike far to find yourself somewhere that feels entirely new as you move through a challenging, yet stunning landscape of rainforests, cliffsides, and mountains. Thickly wooded trails suddenly open up upon vistas that frame gorgeous waterways while hidden away waterfalls are a common and lovely surprise along the majority of paths. Just as you get the hang of an elevation change, the path widens and you're face to face with a glacier. Whether you're excited to stumble upon remnants of a long-ago gold rush or have your heart set on experiencing wildlife in its natural habitat, Juneau is packed with potential for excitement for those that love to get out on foot and make the most of the many trails and camping opportunities just waiting to be discovered.

#42 Perseverance Trail

Coordinates: 58.304506, -134.407167

Experienced hikers looking for a path that blends seamlessly between an urban and natural environment will want to begin their outdoor adventures with a trek along Perseverance Trail. Reaching the trailhead is an exercise that begins in downtown Juneau and has hikers following Basin Road to the canyon that acts as the trail's official starting point. This trail is marked as moderately difficult and includes some stunning scenery ranging from old mine shafts to waterfalls and impressive ridgelines. Get the most out of your hike by approaching the trail as an out and back excursion that's just under 6-miles in total.

#43 Mendenhall Campground

8510 Mendenhall Loop Road, Juneau, Alaska 99801

Camping is an experience in outdoor adventure that brings you close to those you love while providing challenges along the way. When you're on the hunt for the perfect campground in Juneau that brings the outdoor appeal and unbeatable views, make sure to reserve your place at Mendenhall Campground. This highly-popular destination is open to adventurers May through September with availability updates released in November. Situated on the shores of Mendenhall Lake, this campsite comes with an incredible view of the nearby glacier and lies nothing more than a convenient 13-miles from downtown. Whether you arrive in the spirit of tent camping or are enthusiastically pulling up in an RV, Mendenhall Campground has 69 sites to accommodate your trip and time in the wilderness of Juneau.

#44 Alpine Loop Trail

Coordinates: 60.007611, -149.406781

The view at the top of Mount Roberts is spectacular so imagine how thrilling it is for hikers to learn there's much more to be explored on foot once you've disembarked the Mount Roberts Tramway. The Alpine Loop Trail is accessible from the 1,800-foot mark and provides a pristine pathway that lets hikers enjoy an additional 300-foot climb in elevation. The Alpine Loop Trail is known and loved for its many mountaintop vistas, valleys and rocky ridges that never fail to impress. While the scenery is dramatic, this trail is suitable for hikers of all ages and abilities.

#45 Photo Point Trail

Coordinates: 58.4409 N, 134.5459 W

When time is of the essence, but you're in the mood for some impressive scenery and just enough of a physical challenge, make sure to find your way to Photo Point Trail. No more than 1/3 of a mile round trip Photo Point Trail is a tranquil experience that provides beautiful opportunities for photos and is wheelchair accessible as well. Mountainous vistas, thick foliage, and opportunities to encounter a variety of bird species make this popular trail a rather packed place during the summer months. If you're looking for quiet time on the trail, be sure to show up early or choose to trek closer towards the off-season.

#46 East Glacier Loop

Coordinates: 58.417797, -134.543651

When summer is in full swing, it's hard to find a time when the Mendenhall Glacier Visitor Center isn't packed with excited visitors from across the country and globe. If you're looking for a trek that takes you out of the hustle and bustle, head for East Glacier Loop. Covering 3.5-miles of terrain, East Glacier Loop is a lovely hike that provides outdoor adventurers with the opportunity to delve into the heart of the forests that rise above the Mendenhall Valley.

#47 Nugget Creek Trail

8150 Mendenhall Loop Road, Juneau, Alaska 99801

Experienced hikers seeking a more extensive, yet less populated route to traverse will want to make sure to put Nugget Creek Trail on their must-hike list. Nugget Creek Trail covers just under 7.5-miles of land and is an out and back trail that's ideal for mountain biking, running or traditional hiking. The trail can be easily accessed at the Mendenhall Glacier Recreation Area and offers up a path teeming with thick foliage and vegetation to be explored. The majority of hikers choose to end their hike at Vista Creek Shelter.

#48 West Glacier Trail

Coordinates: 58.418336, -134.589999

Where the East Glacier Trail is accessible from the Mendenhall Glacier Visitor Center, the West Glacier Trail is a bit more exclusive and must be accessed from the Mendenhall Campground. At just under 3.5-miles of terrain, the West Glacier Trail is more suited to experienced hikers as it requires some challenging trekking up rocky and rather steep landscapes. The effort is well worth it as the summit of this trail offers up amazing views of the glacier.

#49 Moraine Ecology Trail

Coordinates: 58.417617, -134.565979

The perfect connection trail from the Steep Creek Trail, Moraine Ecology Trail often sees hikers using the Mendenhall Glacier Visitor Center as a starting point. Ducks and loons are frequently spotted in the many ponds that dot this trail while spectacular scenery is always readily available. While the Moraine Ecology Trail is no more than a mile long, it provides hikers with a mossy, forested landscape teeming with wildlife. Be sure to bring your camera on this trail as you're sure to find yourself face to face with breathtaking views of both the glacier and lake.

Chapter 8: Education

When a city such as Juneau experiences significant fluctuation in population due to tourism, it can be easy to begin to see it as a destination designed to deliver on travel memories and less of a permanent residence. For many students and academics, it's the seasonal influx that makes Juneau the perfect place to study, learn and grow. The same landscape that calls to visitors from around the globe intrigues students from just as far away that are looking to learn in a setting that provides the ultimate hands-on environment. There's something spectacular about the prospect of studying for a future career in a place that also provides unsurpassed solitude and community with nature when it's time for exactly that. At a university level, Juneau is an outdoor academic's dream while simultaneously providing instruction in arts and culture that can be carried well beyond the borders of Alaska once a diploma is earned.

For students who call Juneau home from a young age, the opportunity to grow up and earn an education within the boundaries of Southeast Alaska provides some unique and wonderful opportunities otherwise unavailable in the Lower 48. Athletic teams within Juneau travel by ferry frequently to nearby coastal communities in the name of friendly competition. Science classes come to life with students able to find real-life examples sitting outside their classroom door. An emphasis on fragile ecosystems can be witnessed with a walk through Tongass National Forest. For all that makes Juneau an exceptional city for textbook education, it's also earned a reputation as a place where lifelong friendships are forged and important childhood memories are made within the classroom.

#50 The University of Alaska Southeast

11066 Auke Lake Way, Juneau, Alaska 99801

Juneau is a city of natural beauty and endless entertainment, but it's also a destination that prides itself on being an oasis of education and learning. Juneau is home to The University of Alaska Southeast which is part of the greater University of Alaska educational system. This four-year university opened its doors to students in 1987 and has extended locations in both Sitka and Ketchikan. Situated between Auke Lake and Auke Bay, The University of Alaska Southeast welcomes just under 5,000 undergraduate students and just over 500 graduate students on an annual basis. While the university provides programs that focus on everything from business and education to languages, the university's prime location in the Tongass National Forest makes it an academic institution with amazing opportunities for those students pursuing future careers in biology, coastal studies, and social sciences.

#51 Juneau School District

1208 Glacier Avenue, Juneau, Alaska 99801

For those who fall in love with Juneau upon visiting and find themselves considering relocation, it's good to note that the Juneau School District comes with high ratings and recommendations. The Juneau School District is home to over 4,500 elementary, middle and high school aged students on an annual basis. This public school district proudly holds the title of fifth largest in the state of Alaska. Students are placed between six elementary schools, two middle schools, and two high schools. Enrollment is open at the high school level and contrary to many boundary lines drawn by public schools in the lower 48, students in Juneau are free to pick and choose schools according to preference. The Juneau School District is integrated with homeschooling associations and residential youth facilities to accommodate students from all walks of educational life. Language and literacy programs are woven into the curriculum in order to meet the needs of a significant Alaska Native Heritage population

Chapter 9: Romantic Destinations

Juneau is a city that has long-inspired outdoor adventurers to come and try their luck within the mountains, mist, and sea but it just may be these same dramatic and intriguing features that make the city an oasis of romantic potential as well. Whether you're looking to rekindle a romance or simply seeking quality time with the one you love, Juneau provides an exceptional backdrop for amorous escapades in a thrilling setting. For those couples that crave a luxurious getaway complete with oldtown charm and modern amenities and services, there are several bed and breakfast destinations that pamper and cater to guests' every need. Those couples heading to Juneau for time spent together in the great outdoors will find the color, trails, and options for getting out on the open water endlessly exciting. No matter how you spend your time together, Juneau invites couples to come and make memories together in a place quite unlike any other on Earth.

#52 Pearson's Pond Luxury Inn and Adventure Spa

4541 Sawa Circle #1, Juneau, Alaska 99801

Juneau is just the place you need to visit when you're looking to rekindle the romance in an amazing setting. Pearson's Pond Luxury Inn and Adventure Spa brings the upscale resort-style feeling to a bed and breakfast approach to your stay. As soon as you arrive, the ambiance is saturated with warmth and welcome. Tucked into inspiring rainforest scenery, this romantic destination comes complete with a rainforest garden and elegant amenities including Jacuzzi tubs, fireplaces, and ultra-plush bedding. The staff at Pearson's Pond Luxury Inn and Adventure Spa are always on-hand to help guests set up romantic hikes, bikes, and excursions built for two. Once you've spent your day exploring together, make the most of the on-site spa services which include everything from skin treatments to massage. You're sure to leave Pearson's hand in hand, feeling like new.

#53 Alaska's Capital Inn Bed and Breakfast

113 5th Street Stairs, Juneau, Alaska 99801

Charming, rustic and elegant, Alaska's Capital Inn Bed and Breakfast is one of the most romantic places to stay in Juneau for those couples looking to make the most of time together in a setting that embodies the spirit of Southeast Alaska. Comfort and convenience are kept top of mind for guests staying in this meticulously renovated home that has been sitting on a hillside with amazing views since 1906. This gold rush era residence is charming as it is magical. Located near downtown, you never have to travel far for entertainment, but when you're looking to stay in, every comfort in the world. awaits. King beds, local art, and period-specific wallpaper give this destination a delicious turn of the century feel. Cozy up in a room for two or enjoy the outdoors by finding a place on the patio with a drink in hand and mountains rising up on either side.

#54 Glacier Gardens Rainforest Adventure

7600 Glacier Highway, Juneau, Alaska 99801

Couples inspired by color, vibrant scenery and breathtaking designs won't want to miss the opportunity to take part in a guided tour of Glacier Gardens Rainforest Adventure when they're in Juneau. Sprawling over 50-acres of land, this experience takes guests through a sweeping and vast rainforest garden where one of a kind trees, foliage, and flora are display in gorgeous arrangements. While you're here you'll learn about the diverse and essential ecosystems and wildlife that make up the complex Tongass National Forest. While this destination is highly popular with engaged couples looking for the ideal wedding venue, it's just as intriguing for those couples looking to spend a few tranquil hours together in a space of unmatched beauty.

#55 Silverbow Inn-Urban Boutique Hotel

120 2nd Street, Juneau, Alaska 99801

Those couples that find their stride in a setting that offers up the best of modern luxury will want to be sure to reserve their room at the Silverbow Inn when they travel to Juneau. Silverbow Inn is an exclusive establishment downtown that provides guests with the best of upscale modern living in the heart of a setting that's built for outdoor adventures. This boutique hotel is the result of extensive renovation within a historic Juneau landmark building that has resulted in 12 guest rooms equipped with Wi-Fi, rooftop hot tubs and exceptional bed and breakfast service for every stay. Indulge in the mountain scenery from the comfort of a luxurious over-sized bed before ordering an organic breakfast that comes with locally roasted coffee perfect for starting your day in upscale style.

#56 Twin Lakes

3401-3499 Glacier Highway, Juneau, Alaska 99801

If your idea of a romantic getaway revolves around an outdoor adventure in a setting that still supplies plenty of romance, make your way to Twin Lakes for a day of walking along the shore and settling into a kayak or two when the mood strikes. Twin Lakes is a gorgeous area that provides plenty of options for hiking, biking, relaxing or simply taking in the scenery when you're here. Many visitors to Twin Lakes come with a pole and line in hand in the name of a great catch while others come for berry picking when the season is just right. Plan to spend an afternoon or longer when Twin Lakes holds a spot on your romantic itinerary.

Chapter 10: Downtown Landmarks

When it's excitement and the hustle and bustle of life that you crave on vacation, make sure to plan on spending a significant amount of time in downtown Juneau. This central waterfront hub of tourism, business and flavor is where you'll be able to find everything from restaurants and bars to art stores, galleries, sensational statues, and theaters. Downtown is easily accessed from the cruise ship terminal making it a buzzing and busy place to be during the high season summer months. In the winter, downtown transforms into more of a locale for year-round residents who appreciate the calm and conversation that comes along once the cruise ships have left their wake on the horizon. Whether you're looking for the perfect souvenir, hoping to find some savory seafood or looking to enjoy the artistic side of life in Juneau, downtown is a hot spot destination filled with possibilities.

#57 Alaska Pedicab-Juneau

3251 Douglas Highway, Juneau, Alaska 99801

There's no better way to get from place to place in Juneau than by calling Alaska Pedicab. Dialing 907-782-4396 is the easiest way to get in contact with one of the many foot peddlers that arrive to transport Juneau visitors quickly and in an eco-friendly style.

Hop in and enjoy a ride that's as good for the environment as it is for the senses. You'll get a great feel for how downtown and surrounding areas are laid out while getting to your next destination in a timely manner too.

#58 Humpback Whale Statue

Harris Harbor Way, Juneau, Alaska 99801

It's hard to miss this stunning homage to Juneau's most majestic underwater creatures. Rising out of the Gastineau Channel along the Riverwalk, guests are often thrilled to see a life size bronze humpback whale rising out of the water in a full breach. Officially titled Tahku, this amazing statue was designed and constructed in honor of Alaska's 50th year as a state. The sculpture was designed by R.T. Wallen and was created to inspire all Juneau residents and visitors each time it's passed.

#59 Mount Juneau Trading Post

151 S. Franklin Street, Juneau, Alaska 99801

In support of First Nation artists, Mount Juneau Trading Post is a family-run business with Tlingit Nation roots. This store features the work of native artists throughout Alaska from up and coming crafters to those whose names are well-known throughout the state and beyond. From scrimshaws to knives, baskets, and jewelry, Mount Juneau Trading Post displays an endless variety of products that speak to the culture and heritage that has long defined the Last Frontier.

#60 Juneau's Imagination Station

174 A S. Franklin Street, Juneau, Alaska 99801

When you're traveling to Juneau with little ones in tow, there's no better place to stop downtown than Juneau's Imagination Station. This one of a kind toy store is packed with potential souvenirs that kids will fall in love with. Entertaining families since opening in 2003, Juneau's Imagination Station is packed with toys that include dolls, arts and science kits, puzzles, novelty toys and books that educate on all things Alaska. With over 1,600-square feet of toy space available, every child is sure to find that special something that helps them remember their trip to Juneau.

#61 Caribou Crossings

387 S. Franklin Street, Juneau, Alaska 99801

A trip to Juneau is sure to come with its fair share of souvenirs, but there's nothing better than finding a place where local insider information is just as easily accessed as locally crafted jewelry. Caribou Crossings provides this perfect blend of products and information as a downtown destination that's been popular with visitors and locals for over 20-years. Here, visitors can find a variety of hand-crafted goods that display the talent of over 60 local artists while getting some of the most relevant tips from staff that has long called Juneau home. At Caribou Crossings, you can just as easily figure out how to book the best kayaking trip as you can pick up an amazing set of Jade earrings in honor of Alaska's national gemstone.

#62 Gold Town Nickelodeon Theater

171 Shattuck Way #109, Juneau, Alaska 99801

Those visitors to Juneau with a passion for film and a heart for the finer old-fashioned things in life won't want to miss a chance to catch a movie at the Gold Town Nickelodeon Theater while you're here. Complete with wooden fold down seats and accommodating only 80 guests at a time, this throwback theater is a wonderful place to grab some popcorn and enjoy an indie or alternative movie. Quaint, charming and decked out in historically chic décor, Gold Town is a fan favorite for those looking for a fun night out on the town.

#63 Waterfront Spotting Scopes

155 South Seward Street, Juneau, Alaska 99801-Port of Juneau

Even if you're an avid hiker, chances are slim that you'll come face to face with one of Juneau's many mountain goats that call Mt. Juneau home. Agile and instinctive, these rock-climbing creatures are experts when it comes to scaling impossibly steep walls and rock faces at heights that would make most nervous. Instead, turn a distance white speck on the mountain into a captivating encounter with a mountain goat with the help of one of the many spotting scopes located on Juneau's waterfront. Easy to use and an amazing way to get a close up look at these fascinating animals, the spotting scopes are sure to please those who are less inclined to head towards the mountain and are comfortable with their waterfront vantage point.

#64 Alaskan Hotel & Bar

167 S. Franklin Street, Juneau, Alaska 99801

With roots dating back to 1913, the Alaskan Hotel & Bar is a prized historical landmark in Juneau and one of the most exciting stops downtown as well. You don't have to have a reservation to make the most of the nightly live musical performances. While the hotel was designed with Victorian inspiration in mind, the attached bar speaks to gold rush flair and invites guests to come in, grab a spot at a cozy table and enjoy a drink and music too. The central location of the Alaskan Hotel & Bar makes it a favorite for those visitors looking to make the most of all there is to do downtown during their stay.

#65 The Senate Building

175 S. Franklin Street, Juneau, Alaska 99801

Don't be surprised if you hear The Senate Building fondly referred to as The Senate Mall. Perhaps this would be a more accurate name anyway as this historic landmark is known as downtown's prime shopping destination. Built in 1913, The Senate Building holds the title as one of Alaska's oldest historic landmarks but has also been the site of extensive renovations to keep up with changing times since its foundation was first laid. This four-story building is primarily made up of retail space with the top dedicated to offices. Its convenient location puts it within walking distance of the cruise ship terminal making it a popular place to visit for those who are in town for only a few hours or just the day. From fly fishing products to women's apparel and the many Alaskan handcrafted goods in between, the Senate Building hosts a variety of items ready to be purchased when inspiration hits.

#66 The Alaska Steam Laundry

174 S. Franklin Street, Juneau, Alaska 99801

Juneau is intriguing for visitors in the sense that it's just as easy to feel the remnants of gold rush culture as it is to see the innovative steps forward the city has taken since that incredible time in history. One of the best places to view this transition through architecture is The Alaska Steam Laundry downtown. Easy to identify by its castle-like spire and late Victorian façade, The Alaska Steam Laundry housed miners up until 1929. Today it is filled with commercial retail space that accommodates a growing tourist population but the past is still clearly etched on the exterior of this building which was built in 1901 and listed on the National Register of Historic Places in 1978.

#67 Windfall Fisherman Statue

359 Main Street, Juneau, Alaska 99801

The wildlife that inhabits the city of Juneau and the surrounding landscape have long defined this beautiful destination and captivated locals and visitors alike. Of all the creatures that inspire both awe and fear, the Alaskan brown bear reigns supreme. In honor of this powerful animal that calls Alaska home, visitors to Juneau are encouraged to come and admire the Windfall Fisherman statue that sits on Main Street. This life size bronze sculpture of a brown bear is impressive in size and accuracy. Designed by R.T. Wallen, the statue was commissioned to celebrate Alaska's 25-years of statehood and was completed in 1984.

#68 Shoefly Alaska

109 Seward Street, Juneau, Alaska 99801

To make the most of time spent in Juneau, the proper footwear is often required. The team at Shoefly Alaska has perfected the art of providing shoes that are both durable enough to withstand Juneau's weather and terrain while maintaining a sense of style that's undeniable. Many return visitors to Juneau find themselves leaving at least one empty space in their suitcase for a pair of Shoefly Alaska favorites. Whether you stop in once or come back year after year, the selection is impressive and the styles one of a kind.

#69 Alaska Shirt Company

489 S. Franklin Street, Juneau, Alaska 99801

When you're in need of an Alaskan-inspired souvenir or two, there's no place quite like the Alaska Shirt Company. Sitting proudly just off the cruise ship terminal, this one-stop shop offers up everything from glacier-themed t-shirts to Ulu knives and the many keychains in between. Started by six friends with a passion for everything Alaska, the Alaska Shirt Company provides a warm and welcoming atmosphere for those with a goal of landing on just the right item to remember their trip by.

Chapter 11: Culture and Heritage

A modern city is always an intricate collection of its many historical stories. Juneau's past is one that is steeped in Native Heritage and a visit to Alaska's capital brings with it ample opportunity to explore, learn and experience these captivating cultures for one's self. From the Sealaska Heritage Institute to the museums that work hard to capture and preserve a traditional way of life, maintaining a sense of understanding and awareness around the Native cultures of Juneau is essential to the city's very heartbeat. While indigenous tribes inhabited Southeast Alaska as early as 10,000 years ago, Juneau is home to the Haida, Tsimshian, and Tlingit, all three of which maintain a strong voice and presence throughout the city today. Overall, there is a sense amongst Juneau city officials and residents that a continued understanding surrounding diversity is key to moving the city forward in the modern world. In the spirit of spreading the word of culture and acceptance, Juneau is home to an incredible bi-annual festival that brings the masses together in the name of culture, heritage, and tradition.

While Native Heritage is strong in Juneau, the city has a lot to say in the way of its political and religious history as well. Those interested in getting a closer look at Juneau's journey within Alaska from territory to state will appreciate time spent at the Alaska State Museum and the Governor's Mansion. As it pertains to the integration of religion through the city, a stop at both St. Nicholas and Cathedral of the Nativity is a wonderful way to learn how faith has long played a part in Juneau's modern story. The city's history is rich in gold and several museums work to showcase the pioneers that came to Juneau in search of wealth during the gold rush era. Guests can even play the part by visiting an old gold mine and mill for a hands-on look at the steps required to discover, mine and mill the gold that could potentially launch a pioneer into a new social status based on their pocketbook alone. Whether your time in Juneau focuses on indigenous heritage or look more closely at how the gold rush shaped the city we know and love today, it's not hard to see from the moment you arrive that culture and heritage are values held close for the people that call this city their own.

#70 Sealaska Heritage Institute

105 South Seward Street, Juneau, Alaska 99801

Just as diverse as Juneau's physical landscape is the array of native peoples that called this destination home long before it was known as Juneau. Those looking to gain a better understanding of Juneau's rich cultural story will want to make time for a visit to the Sealaska Heritage Institute. As a private nonprofit, the Sealaska Heritage Institute was founded in 1980 and today continues to grow and expand as a place where history is celebrated and education and cultural diversity is continuously promoted. Programs, art shows, public events, and services all work to highlight the Tsimshian, Haida and Tlingit cultures that continue to call Southeast Alaska home.

#71 Alaska State Museum

395 Whittier Street, Juneau, Alaska 99801

Culture, history, and geography are all highlighted through a series of meticulously curated displays and exhibits for those interested in visiting the Alaska State Museum. Featuring displays that cover topics pertaining to both natural and human history, the Alaska State Museum houses over 32,000 relevant artifacts that range from preserved specimen to Alaska native art. Historical exhibits move seamlessly through the importance of the many native groups in this area on through Russian colonialism as well as the gold rush, mining culture and modern approaches to tourism, transportation, economy, and commerce.

#72 Governor's Mansion

716 Calhoun Avenue, Juneau, Alaska 99801

The trek uphill from central downtown is worth the effort for those interested in politics, history, and architecture. Your uphill walk reveals the Governor's Mansion which was originally built in 1913 and remains as impressive today as it once was with its stark white façade and beautifully detailed totem pole rising into the sky. A sprawling balcony adorns the exterior of this historic and political landmark while the inside of the home hosts an incredible 26 rooms.

#73 St. Nicholas

326 5th Street, Juneau, Alaska 99801

Officially known as the St. Nicholas Orthodox Church, this religious landmark is an incredible stop in Juneau and is easily identified by it's gorgeous white and blue façade. Built in 1893, St. Nicholas continues to be a primary place of worship for those practicing the Russian Orthodox faith. The church was founded in Juneau by the Tlingit people who had met with Bishop Nikolai Ziorov in July of 1982 and were enthralled by his religious message. With over 125-years of history behind it, it comes as no surprise that this destination was listed on the National Register of Historic Places in 1973.

#74 Cathedral of the Nativity

416 5th Street, Juneau, Alaska 99801

Referenced formally as Cathedral of the Nativity of the Blessed Virgin Mary, this church holds the title as Mother Church of the Roman Catholic community in Juneau. Compared to soaring cathedrals elsewhere in the lower 48, the Cathedral of the Nativity is quaint, but well situated within the scenery of Juneau. Visitors are invited to come to participate in daily mass or simply admire the sacred artwork that is housed in the cathedral. Stunning and vibrant stained-glass windows bring Biblical stories to life in this house of worship while providing the interior with an ethereal effect that's undeniably beautiful.

#75 Evergreen Cemetery

601 Seater Street, Juneau, Alaska 99801

Just as important as finding innovative paths to modernity is a city's ability to honor the past. This goal is achieved beautifully at Juneau's Evergreen Cemetery. Sprawling across 10-acres of land, Evergreen Cemetery was established in 1887 and is the final resting place of some of the most important historical figures in Juneau's story. City founder Joe Juneau and co-founder Richard Harris are both laid to rest in this cemetery as well as famous pioneer John Olds and Mayor Waino Edward Hendrickson just to name a few. Meticulously maintained pathways lead through lush lawns where headstones can be admired for their age, beauty and artistic value as well. A plot mapping project was successfully completed for the cemetery in 2015 by the Parks and Recreation Department making it simple for family, friends or visitors to this destination to locate specific graves.

#76 The Federal Building

709 W. 9th Street, Juneau, Alaska 99801

Alaska officially became a state in 1959 and the 1960s saw stunning structural growth throughout the capital of Juneau. These progressive and often impressive feats of architecture were meant to be steps forward in Alaska's new identity, but also pave the way for future growth as well. The Federal Building's construction began in 1962 and was completed in 1966. It was designed as a symbol of Alaska's new place in the U.S. and a point of pride for many who called Juneau home. Today, the Federal Building houses laboratories and a variety of federal agencies including the Postal Service and National Park Service to name a few. It sits pristinely within the boundaries of the historic Casey-Shattuck neighborhood, only six blocks west of downtown making it an easy stroll for visitors dropped off at the cruise ship terminal.

#77 Juneau-Douglas City Museum

114 W. 4th Street, Juneau, Alaska 99801

The cultural heritage of Southeast Alaska takes center stage for visitors to the Juneau-Douglas City Museum. Housed in the former Juneau Memorial Library with roots dating back to 1951, this museum is a wonderful way to spend an afternoon immersed in the history, stories and people that have made Juneau the dynamic destination it is today. While the museum welcomes a diverse lineup of new and revolving exhibits, the permanent collection is wonderfully impressive and comprehensive. Permanent galleries highlight Juneau's changing shoreline, Tlingit culture, and history, mining, politics, and topography. The museum hosts several public and educational events throughout the year and is most notably the location of the 1959 Statehood Ceremony.

#78 Last Chance Mining Museum

1001 Basin Road, Juneau, Alaska 99801

Those who call Juneau home are well aware that it's a city that was born and built on the discovery of gold. As Joe Juneau made his way into the area, it was the prospect of shimmering natural discoveries and unimaginable wealth that led to Juneau becoming a place people flocked. As a result, hard rock gold mining was a way of life. From 1912 until 1944, the Alaska Juneau Gold Mining Company operated out of an off-the-beaten-path building that today has been transformed into the Last Chance Mining Museum. Mining for hard rock gold went well beyond the often assumed shake pan and stream. This laborious endeavor involved the use of vast air compressors as well as locomotives and rail cars to transport material to mills. Visitors to the Last Chance Mining Museum will enjoy the opportunity to get an up-close look at these diverse tools that were once used to unearth the hidden treasures Juneau's land held. General admission to this museum is only $5 and private and group tours are available upon request.

#79 House of Wickersham

213 7th Street, Juneau, Alaska 99801

As gold was discovered in and around Juneau, new residents mostly made up of pioneer gold miners flooded into town. While the prospect of wealth was intriguing, the large influx in population also saw a rise amongst criminal acts when growth went unchecked alongside law. James Wickersham is credited with bringing order, progress and potential to not only Juneau but the entire state of Alaska during his time serving both Congress and as a federal judge. This multi-faceted individual was known as a historian, scholar and esteemed author in addition to his many contributions to laws that would go on to govern Juneau and Alaska into a state of order and compliance in the midst of tremendous growth.

Working extensively on criminal and civil codes that would benefit the people of Alaska, Jude Wickersham purchased what was known as The House on the Ridge in 1928 and lived there until his death in 1939. The House on the Ridge was originally built in 1898 and had long housed some of Juneau's most highly-regarded residents. With his passing, The House on the Ridge was lovingly renamed House of Wickersham and was purchased by The State of Alaska in 1984. Today it functions as a museum and houses photographs, artifacts and period-specific furniture that speaks to the years Wickersham spent dedicating his time and energy to helping Juneau and all of Alaska thrive.

#80 A-J Mine

500 Sheep Creek Mine Road, Juneau, Alaska 99801

Hearing about the impact of gold mining on the city of Juneau is one thing, seeing where it actually happened is another experience altogether. Visitors to Juneau have the opportunity to get into the heart of gold mining by booking a guided tour through A-J Mine when they're here. Before it was the largest gold mining site in Juneau, the A-J Mine began as a small dig site in 1913. The mine's overall construction was divided into four sections over the course of two years that allowed for the development of a sturdy foundation and convenient transportation of materials for miners.

A-J Mine ran successfully up until World War I when the vast majority of miners were called into military service. The cost of gold after the war made it unprofitable for workers to return and the mine was officially closed in 1921. Today, guests can follow a knowledgeable guide through what remains of the mine using hard hats and lights to safely navigate a 360-foot long tunnel. Demonstrations highlighting mining tools and equipment are followed up by a trip back to the mill where guests can try panning for themselves.

#81 Walter Soboleff Building

105 S. Seward Street, Juneau, Alaska 99801

The Walter Soboleff Building houses the greater Sealaska Heritage Institute and is a cultural icon in the city of Juneau. Guests to this meaningful and educational destination of cultural diversity are invited to stop in and explore a variety of exhibits that highlight native culture through a Native lens. Art displays as well as an opportunity to see an authentic clan house make a trip to the Walter Soboleff Building truly remarkable. Before you leave, you'll want to make sure to stop in at the Sealaska Heritage store where Native handcrafted art is available for purchase alongside souvenirs and gifts to commemorate your trip. Profits earned from the sale of these goods is directed back towards supporting cultural events and programs in Juneau.

#82 Celebration

105 S. Seward Street, Juneau, Alaska 99801

Long before pioneers made their way to the Northwest Coast, tribes that called this area home thrived within the landscape and within their vibrant culture and customs. As settlements began appearing across Juneau and the entirety of Southeast Alaska, it became more important than ever for Native groups to hold tightly to their culture, customs, and traditions. Today, this is as true as it was hundreds of years ago. Every other June in Juneau, the Sealaska Heritage Institute plays host to Celebration which holds the title as the second largest gathering of Alaska Natives in the state. Over the course of four days, the Tsimshian, Haida, and Tlingit come together to honor and highlight the many dances, foods, arts and music that have long defined their individual cultures and tribes. Native languages are spoken, performances abound and in all, it is estimated that Celebration draws in approximately 5,000 participants which doesn't include over 2,000 dancers that come to showcase talents and tradition. For Alaska Native groups, Celebration is a new tradition to be added to a long lineup of rich history. For those that come to appreciate and observe the ceremonies, it is an educational experience quite unlike any other and an amazing look into the culture and tribes that have long defined the city and surrounding lands that make up Juneau.

#83 Aunt Claudia's Dolls

114 S. Franklin Street #102, Juneau, Alaska 99801

Over the course of her lifetime, Juneau resident Claudia Kelsey collected over 800 dolls including a vast array of manuscripts, articles, and research surrounding the significance of dolls, particularly to Alaska Native groups. Upon her passing, Aunt Claudia's Dolls was opened as a public museum where Claudia Kelsey's collection was meticulously recreated as it had been in her home and a display space and library were added to the floorplan. Today, the museum is open to visitors looking for a unique take on their visit to Juneau. While the original collection is still impressive, with the help of contributors over the years it's grown significantly into a breathtaking exhibit of miniatures, dolls, and toys from around the world. While collectors are often fascinated with a stop at Aunt Claudia's Dolls, it's a very family-friendly museum that inspires children to take a closer look at what it means to collect. Current curator and host Mary Ellen Frank maintains a doll studio in the museum where she practices the art of doll making much to the delight of visitors looking for a closer look at how these treasures come together from the very beginning.

#84 Annie Kaill's

124 Seward Street, Juneau, Alaska 99801

Juneau's stunning natural landscape and dynamic terrain make it a place that has long inspired artists from near and far to capture its beauty through mixed mediums. Since first opening its doors to the public in 1975, Annie Kaill's has been a downtown Juneau destination that has provided a space for local art to be exhibited as well as available for purchase. Annie Kaill's displays a wide variety of local artwork including jewelry, pottery, glassware, paintings and more. Feel free to stop in and simply browse the beautiful pieces on display or take time to show up when the gallery comes to life with the work of up and coming talent. Annie Kaill's prides itself on being a place where young artists can get their name and works out into the public in the very place that inspires their creativity.

#85 Juneau Artists Gallery Ltd.

175 S. Franklin Street #111, Juneau, Alaska 99801

As the city of Juneau continues to grow with time, many businesses that were once exclusively seasonal find themselves in the prosperous position of being able to transition to year-round companies that thrive. Juneau Artists Gallery Ltd. is a prime example of this growth and a beacon of innovation that has continued to flourish since it's opening in 1985. The gallery is owned and operated by 23 artists who hail from Juneau and use the space to not only display their own work but to encourage other artists to join the team and do the same. This corporation provides an opportunity for local artists to gain membership into the Juneau Artists Gallery and upon achieving this status, a designated display space is provided. From here, the opportunities are seemingly endless. Member artists are invited to act as independent curators of their space and have complete creative reign over their displays. In addition, each Juneau Artists Gallery member is involved in the daily operation of the gallery which includes helping plan special events, open houses, attending monthly meetings and working towards the continued growth and prosperity of the gallery.

#86 Alaska Robotics Gallery

220 Front Street, Juneau, Alaska 99801

When it comes to creativity, Juneau locals have always had a knack for combining the best of traditional inspiration and the satire that adds a bit of edge to artistry. Alaska Robotics Gallery was started by a group of friends looking to promote the creative culture of Juneau while also taking aim at Alaskan politics. What began as a team effort to produce short films and comics that were made to entertain and highlight issues in politics has since grown to be an effort that mobilizes Juneau youth in the name of artistic endeavors. While the Alaska Robotics Gallery on Front Street carries everything from local music to graphic novels and film, it's also a wonderful place to pick up local artwork and souvenirs. More recently, the Alaska Robotics Gallery has extended into city-wide events. In 2016, Alaska Robotics hosted its first mini-comic convention in Juneau which doubled as an artist camp over the course of five fun-filled days.

#87 Wilderness Peaks Gallery

159 S. Franklin Street, Juneau, Alaska 99801

Those travelers to Juneau with a passion for photography won't want to miss the chance to visit Wilderness Peaks Gallery. This artistic haven is home to photographs that feature the work of photographer Daniel Buck who spends the majority of his time capturing the beauty and stunning diversity of Southeast Alaska's incredible terrain. While he's traveled the world over in pursuit of images that capture the delicate balance between urban and natural beauty, an adventurous spirit has long connected him to Juneau and Southeast Alaska where he has found some of his most inspiring shots come to life. Whether it's the glimmering blue top of a glacier or mesmerizing mountainsides that are unspeakably steep his works speak to a more intimate relationship with nature. Juneau provides a stunning backdrop for photographers who will inevitably find the collection of works at Wilderness Peaks Gallery endlessly inspiring.

#88 State Office Noon Concert

333 Willoughby Avenue, Juneau, Alaska 99801

As with so many things in life, it's often the unexpected surprises in Juneau that make for the best travel memories. While there's no guarantee, those lucky enough to stumble upon a noon concert at the State Office Building during their trip will be entitled to an event they won't soon forget. While it's normally seated safely behind glass, every once in a while, the Kimball pipe organ that was originally designed in 1928 by Alaska theater owner W.D. Gross comes to life in the name of classical music made for the masses to enjoy. While the organ was originally donated to the State Museum, it quickly became clear that unlike other historical artifacts, an organ of vast size and splendor is best preserved when it's put to good use. The organ's current home at the State Office makes it just as easy to display as it is to play. Hosting 548 pipes, the organ turns the lobby into a symphony hall under the hands of skilled musicians. While organized performances happen in spurts throughout the year, the busy cruise ship season in Juneau sees the organ's keys requested by onboard musicians who are looking to delight and entertain crowds over the noon hour.

Chapter 12: Conservation Efforts

Juneau is arguably one of the most diverse cities on the map when it comes to landscapes, wildlife, and intricate ecosystems. With such a dynamic landscape making up the city itself, it's not surprising that both the population and number of tourists flooding into Juneau has increased year over year. With the ever-increasing interest in this enchanting destination comes a renewed urgency to protect and preserve the environment that continues to intrigue people from near and far. Juneau is proud to host a number of conservation groups and organizations who have made it their mission to promote the land and creatures they love while promoting awareness amongst locals and visitors. In the spirit of doing what needs to be done today to keep Juneau thriving tomorrow, these groups have become an important part of Juneau's society and an increasingly clear voice amongst the masses who are looking to experience this amazing, yet fragile natural landscape for themselves.

#89 Marine Conservation Alliance

2 Marine Way #227, Juneau, Alaska 99801

Where science, seafood, and sustainability collide, the Marine Conservation Alliance finds its traction in Juneau. This organization is made up of a collection of harvesters, processors, fishing communities and community development representatives looking for a balance between marine habitats, growing populations, and responsible fishing practices. The group aims to prevent overfishing in the waters of Southeast Alaska while simultaneously keeping the fishing industry afloat in a practical and safe manner. Built on a foundation of long-term sustainability goals, the Marine Conservation Alliance in Juneau is an active voice in the community and prides itself on its status as a seafood-interest organization.

#90 Macaulay Salmon Hatchery

2697 Channel Drive, Juneau, Alaska 99801

Salmon has long been a vital and integral part of Southeast Alaska's marine culture providing sustenance for people and animals alike. From daunting salmon runs to large scale fishing operations, salmon are seen at the center of many debates and discussions surrounding the sustainability of fishing on off the coast of Alaska. The Macaulay Salmon Hatchery provides a place for the salmon population to continue to thrive while also acting as an education center for those looking into the importance of this species in the waters surrounding Juneau. Visitors to the Macaulay Salmon Hatchery have the chance to learn about the salmon spawning process from start to finish with the help of a friendly and knowledgeable on-site guide. A sky bridge provides the perfect vantage point for visitors to observe the rearing facility where young Coho and King salmon get their start. Further opportunities to interact with marine life happen when guests continue on to explore the aquarium that features over 150 underwater creatures. Admissions proceeds at Macaulay Salmon Hatchery go towards future educational programs that highlight salmon enhancement in Southeast Alaska.

#91 Southeast Alaska Conservation Council

224 Gold Street, Juneau, Alaska 99801

For over 40 years, the Southeast Alaska Conservation Council has been an important voice when it comes to speaking on the topic of sustainable salmon fishing and protecting an ever-fragile environment that dominates Southeast Alaska. The council consists of scientists, hunters, fishermen, Native Tribes, locals and business professionals who have a heart for all that's natural, good and sustainable in Southeast Alaska. The group looks to create an environment of change through three separate strategic paths. These include the Tongass Forest Program, the Inside Passage Waters Program, and the Grassroots Legal Program. Where the Tongass Forest Program focuses on preserving carbon-rich forests amidst climate change and growing tourism, the Inside Passage Waters Program takes aim at rivers and estuaries of the Inside Passage. The Grassroots Legal Program is made up of professionals that are on-hand to help local communities take on legal and scientific concerns in an effective and helpful manner.

#92 Oceana

175 S. Franklin Street #418, Juneau, Alaska 99801

Developed in 1999, Oceana is a conservation effort that focuses exclusively on restoring the world's oceans in an effort to feed people across the globe. Using a platform of science-based campaigns, Oceana aims to have 30 percent of the world's waterways protected by 2030 in an effort to feed nearly 1 billion people a seafood-based diet on a daily basis. Oceana functions on the combined efforts of scientists, business professionals, fishing communities, community development representatives and donations from supporters around the globe. The potential for feeding the world is as vast as the ocean itself, but sustainability is key and Oceana works to promote awareness aimed at helping others understand the importance of keeping our oceans healthy while restoring decimated marine life populations.

Chapter 13: Day Trips from Juneau

While there's plenty to see and do in Juneau, part of what makes this capital city so special is its place along the Inside Passage. This zigzagging collection of islands is well worth exploring if you have the luxury of time. While it may require some planning to make sure ferries will be ready to go when it's time to head out in the name of adventure, the opportunity to visit, experience and indulge in these striking coastal communities is a chance you won't want to miss.

#93 Alaska Marine Highway System

13485 Glacier Highway, Juneau, Alaska 99801

Visiting Juneau comes with its fair share of creative logistics but the same could be said for reaching all of Alaska's coastal communities. This sprawling state is divided by mountains and sea, making it tricky to travel anywhere on a direct route. The state of Alaska's solution to getting from place to place the most efficiently began to take shape in 1948 and today comes in the form of the Alaska Marine Highway System.

Commonly referred to as the Alaska State Ferry, this waterway system covers over 3,500 miles using a fleet that can accommodate travelers, small vehicles, RV's and freight containers. This year-round transportation service allows Alaska residents and visitors to access more than 35 coastal communities that might otherwise be impossible to reach. While day trips allow for easy movement between communities that are rather close, the ferry system is the best way for visitors to reach distant communities over the course of several days with opportunities to take in the amazing scenery along the way. Vehicles are driven onto the ferry at various ports of call and simply driven off when the final destination is reached. This mode of transportation is popular amongst visitors looking to cover a lot of land during a single trip using an RV or simple camper.

#94 Douglas Island

You only have to cross a single bridge to get from Juneau to Douglas Island, making it the perfect day trip destination when you're looking to add a bit of diversity to your Alaska experience. Douglas Island sits west of Juneau's bustling downtown and is separated from mainland Juneau by the Gastineau Channel. The Juneau-Douglas Bridge is charged with transporting residents between the mainland and Douglas Island and consequently sees heavy traffic on a daily basis. Named for Anglican Bishop John Douglas, Douglas Island provides its very own set of activities and adventures waiting to be discovered. The island can be divided into two sections consisting of Downtown Douglas Island and North Douglas Island. Downtown is home to landmark locations such as Douglas Harbor and Sandy Beach while the north side of the island is known for housing the Eaglecrest Ski Area as well as a helipad popular with sightseeing and tour companies. With an eclectic collection of bars, restaurants and local hangouts, Douglas Island is well worth a visit when you're heading to Juneau.

#95 Ketchikan

Popular on many cruise routes and sitting on the scenic Inside Passage, Ketchikan is an intriguing destination that provides a small town feel alongside rich culture. Ketchikan is known for its many beautiful totem poles speaking to a strong Alaska Native tradition and is also home to the Tongass Historical Museum and Totem Heritage Center. Those who have a heart for the mist and rain will quickly fall in love with the city of Ketchikan which sees more annual rainfall than Juneau. Mountains, waterfalls, and streams make up the breathtaking scenery of Ketchikan which is a city that just over 8,000 residents called home year-round as of 2017.

Many travelers find their way to Ketchikan while seeking a close-up encounter with Misty Fjord National Monument which lies just 22 miles east of city center and is accessible by floatplane. Misty Fjord National Monument encompasses nearly every natural landmark a traveler could imagine when setting off to experience the authentic heart of Southeast Alaska. Covering over 2.2-million acres, this area is home to glaciers, snowy mountain peaks, fjords and stunning waterfalls just waiting to be discovered. Photographers regularly make their way to Ketchikan in the hopes of capturing amazing images of the many eagles, wolves, and bears that call this part of Southeast Alaska home.

Interestingly enough, for all the water Southeast Alaska hosts, Ketchikan is home to the only commercial snorkeling opportunity in the area. Snorkel Alaska offers snorkeling excursions off Mountain Point for groups of up to 25 people at a time. If you're up for some incredible underwater adventure, be prepared to come face to face with jellyfish, sea cucumbers and of course, the ever-present kelp that keeps the many ecosystems in these waters thriving. While the waters around Ketchikan can reach 65 degrees Fahrenheit by the middle of summer, there's no need to worry about fluctuating temperatures. Wetsuits and the necessary snorkeling equipment required to enjoy time in the water are provided to paying guests who choose to do this tour while visiting the city.

If you're in Ketchikan to find just the right souvenir, you don't have to look much further than Creek Street Shops. This boardwalk of commerce comes with a significant amount of charm and plenty of options for browsing handcrafted Alaskan goods. These locally owned shops provide visitors with everything from books and jewelry to pottery and glassware for purchase. When shopping has left you with an appetite, both The Waterfront Restaurant on Tongass Avenue and Alava's Fish-n-Chowder on Water Street come highly recommended for satisfying the taste buds in no time at all.

#96 Chichagof Island

Boasting over 2,000 square miles of land, Chichagof Island is an incredibly scenic destination within the Alaska panhandle. While the natural beauty of this destination is memorable, it may be the bears that make a visit unforgettable. Chichagof Island is home to the most significant number of bears recorded anywhere on earth. The powerful Grizzly is a common sight on Chichagof Island making it a place best explored alongside an experienced outdoor guide for those new to the area. The island was named after Russian explorer Admiral Vasili Chichagov and is incorporated into the greater Tongass National Forest.

#97 Sitka

For those travelers looking to expand on their hiking, fishing and overall exploration opportunities, Sitka is a wonderful city that doesn't take long to reach from Juneau. Spread across Chichagof and Baranof Island, Sitka makes the most of a beautiful landscape, dynamic history, and cultural influences. Sitka is home to the Alaska Raptor Center as well as the Sitka National Historical Park which features a maze of trails for hiking enthusiasts as well as gorgeous and intricate totem poles. Steep mountains, stunning waterways and an array of wildlife make this an incredible destination for those looking for closer encounters with nature, or opportunities to photograph the intrinsic beauty of Southeast Alaska. Whether you have a heart for history, culture, nature or restaurants that speak to bold flavors, Sitka has a little something for everyone.

As a city of just over 9,000 year-round residents, a visit to Sitka comes with the added bonus of a small town feel with big-city potential for fun. If you're not sure where to begin, start your visit to Sitka at the Harrigan Centennial Hall on Harbor Drive where you'll find a welcoming visitor center waiting to meet you. Friendly staff are ready at a moment's notice to offer up incredible historical facts, advice on where to explore and of course, plenty of options for delicious dining experiences while you're here. If you need a bit more history before you get out and dig into the modern version of Sitka, the Sitka Historical Museum sits just next door and provides a comprehensive look at Sitka's past with a focus on the influence of Tlingit culture. If you're looking for budget-friendly stops, this is the one to choose as admission is only $2 per person.

When you're traveling through Sitka with children and need an indoor destination to recuperate while the little ones burn off energy learning, decide to spend some time at the Sitka Sound Science Center on Lincoln Street. This family-fun destination is open Monday through Saturday and highlights marine culture and the importance of fisheries through a variety of intriguing displays and exhibits. Children will love the touch tank for a more hands-on approach to underwater encounters.

Those travelers making their way to Sitka in the summer will want to be sure to check the city calendar to line up their trip with the Sitka Summer Music Festival. While this event is extremely profitable for the city, it's an absolute delight for classical music lovers who come to see the amazing talent featured on several stages over the course of a week. Artists arrive from around Alaska and the globe to make the most of this amazing opportunity that's pleasing for guests and a great way for up and coming artists to test their talent on a larger scale.

#98 Hoonah

Just 30-miles west of Juneau lies the small and charming city of Hoonah. With a population of just under 800 year-round residents, Hoonah makes for an exceptional day trip for those looking to experience off the beaten path beauty in Southeast Alaska. Hoonah is home to Icy Straight Point where whale watching and bear spotting are almost always guaranteed. Misty Bay Lodge and Hoonah Harbor prove to be scenic spots in this quaint city where it's just as easy to spend time admiring the view as it is to be captivated by the unexpected wildlife that shows up along the way. The city of Hoonah is proud to be home to the largest population of Tlingit in Alaska and the close ties to traditional values makes Hoonah an exceptional destination where authentic tribal roots are visible in everyday life. Whether you come for the impressive zip lining opportunities or are interested in understanding more about Alaska Native culture, Hoonah brings the best of small-town Alaska to visitors with each and every visit.

#99 Admiralty Island

It's hard to think of Juneau without associating this destination with bears. Of all the places to see these incredibly powerful and fascinating creatures, Admiralty Island stands out from the pack. The thriving salmon population of Southeast Alaskan waterways means bears of all species find plenty of sustenance in this part of the state. Admiralty Island is part of the greater Alexander Archipelago and houses the Pack Creek Bear Viewing Area which is one of the ultimate destinations for those looking to get a closer encounter with brown bears during their travels. The viewing area is situated on the northeast corner of the island which comfortably plays host to more brown bears than one could find in all of the lower 48. In fact, it is estimated that Admiralty Island is home to over 1,600 brown bears meaning you never have to look far when you're hoping to spot on this incredible island. Admiralty Island sits only 40-miles from Juneau making it a highly accessible day trip destination by kayak, boat or float plane.

#100 Taku Glacier Lodge

This full-day experience is best when booked with Wings Airways which provides direct access via float plane as well as a comprehensive tour of Taku Glacier Lodge for guests. Taku Glacier Lodge sits in the Tongass National Forest and was originally built in 1923 by Dr. Harry C. DeVighne. It was designed to be Alaska's premier fishing and hunting lodge and a destination to house guests looking to explore the

Alaskan wilderness. Today, Taku Glacier Lodge maintains its adventurous appeal and is operated by a team of on-site and live-in staff who welcome guests to this incredible destination. Tour groups to Taku Glacier Lodge leave from downtown Juneau on a floatplane and have the opportunity to view glaciers, waterways, and mountains as they make their way to the lodge. Upon arrival, guests are invited to enjoy a Wild Alaskan salmon dinner cooked over an Alderwood fire. Scenic, breathtaking and delicious, a trip to Taku Glacier Lodge provides the views, flavor, and fun that visitors to Southeast Alaska are craving.

#101 Skagway

Situated along the Inside Passage, the city of Skagway is a popular destination on the cruise ship route and sees its population triple and beyond during the busy summer months. Skagway was a city that thrived during the Klondike Gold Rush years in Southeast Alaska and today guests come to enjoy the gold rush era architecture that still remains. Skagway is home to the Klondike Gold Rush National Historical Park and is a familiar site for those taking a ride on The White Pass and Yukon Route Railroad. Incredible mountain views and impossibly steep cliffsides carry passengers from Skagway up towards Canada where they can view the remnants of gold mines and excavation efforts from the past along with stunning photo opportunities. While Skagway effectively shuts down to tourism in the winter, summer brings out the absolute best of this Southeast gem of a destination.

Those looking to enjoy a convenient day of fun will love Skagway for its comprehensive layout. Guests can truly enjoy a variety of downtown activities that span no more than eight city blocks conveniently located next to the cruise ship terminal. Those jumping on the train for an afternoon ride will find the departure point just as close to the dock, making it an easy excursion for those with any type of mobility issue. After you've had the chance to ride the rails in Skagway, don't forget to get your picture taken by one of the vintage railcars displayed just steps away from the cruise ship terminal.

If you're looking for more history to add to your travels, try stopping by the Skagway City Museum on Spring Street where Native relics, railroad artifacts, and Gold Rush memorabilia abound much to the delight of those with a passion for pursuing the past. For those visitors who are craving some serious time as a consumer, make your way directly to Broad Street. This length of road is packed with locally owned stores that sell everything from postcards and keychains to handcrafted Alaskan art, pottery, and jewelry too. When hunger pains find their way into your day, breakfast is served at the Sweet Tooth Café on Broadway while Starfire Thai Food on Spring and 4th is sure to satisfy those with a hankering for something more robust and exotic.

Chapter 14: Last Minute Tips and Tricks

Being a Mindful Tourist

Take nothing but memories, leave nothing but footprints has long been the motto of mindful travelers everywhere and perhaps it's never more important to remember then when you're traveling to Juneau. This land of glaciers, mountains, wildlife, and incredible Native history is dynamic and equally fragile to degradation as the number of visitors rises with each passing year. While it's encouraging to see the massive number of people interested in experiencing the beauty and unique landscape Juneau offers, it makes it that much more important for visitors to be aware of how their presence affects that natural balance that Juneau heavily relies on to thrive.

Research Before Reaching Your Destination

The rise in the number of cruise ships landing at Juneau's terminal each year is directly associated with the number of tour groups looking to offer services to incoming visitors. From floatplane trips to glacier hikes, dog sledding experiences to whale watching cruises, it's imperative that guests take time to research the company they are planning on exploring with prior to docking at the Port of Juneau. Being environmentally-minded is a wonderful and caring way to approach a trip that focuses so much on the great outdoors. Taking time to look into a company's certifications, safety record and longevity in the field should always be top of mind when it comes to personal safety for any and all excursions in Juneau.

It's also as important for guests to make the time to look into what a tour company does to protect the environment it highlights on its many journeys. Whale watching tours that place a priority on whale conservation will always operate boats that are free from dangerous propellers. While the cost of utilizing these types of vessels is steep for companies, those that do prove time and again that the safety of marine mammals is a top priority. Kayaking excursions will be capped at a certain number of participants per vessel in accordance with safety laws while helicopter tours and floatplane excursions should always come with proof of pilot certification and clear weight and safety restrictions.

Stay Seasonally Savvy

Understanding the seasonal transitions associated with a visit to Juneau can only make you a savvier traveler overall. Southeast Alaska, in general, considers high tourism season to be between May and late September. Those who book trips during this period of time will likely have to deal with more impressive crowds, but will also be privy to experiencing the absolute best of Juneau's wildlife viewing, community services, weather, and tours. Because the seasons determine so much for travelers in Southeast Alaska, it's advisable to make reservations for accommodations and even highly-popular tours as early as 6-months in advance of your travels. The same can be said when it comes to making plans to arrive with a vehicle in tow. While the Alaska Marine Ferry runs frequently, those planning on bringing a car, truck or RV to Juneau will want to make sure they are booked early in order to make sure there are no obstacles to getting your mode of transportation where it needs to go.

Those looking to avoid crowds while still making the most of a trip to Juneau may be more pleasantly surprised by booking in the off-season. Prices are decidedly lower all-around for lodging and tours, but travelers should be willing to work with fewer options as many businesses close during these months as owners take to warmer climates to continue the seasonal business.

Realize the Power of Nature

No matter how experienced an outdoor enthusiast you happen to be, it's important to always give Mother Nature the respect she deserves when traveling throughout Southeast Alaska. Juneau is an urban center and state capital that comes with plenty of entertainment, bold flavors to be discovered and amazing views to soak up, but it's also home to an impressive number of wild creatures. While it's not guaranteed that you'll spot a bear while you're here, understanding the high potential for an encounter and knowing how to respond is the best way to keep yourself safe during your travels. If you happen to be arriving by cruise ship, chances are you'll have the option to attend a seminar or two on what to expect at your port of call. These are worth your time to attend even if your time in Juneau is limited to a day or even a few hours. If you're an independent traveler looking to make the most of hiking, biking and exploring it's important to prepare yourself accordingly. Being able to identify the type of bears that call Juneau home is the first step in preparing for potential and unexpected meet up's out in the wild. Having a clear idea of how to avoid bears is important while knowing how to defend yourself on the trail will give you peace of mind in the event you do come across one of these amazing, yet territorial creatures in their natural habitat.

Just as visitors to Juneau should always recognize the beauty and danger of wild animal encounters, it's just as imperative that guests to this incredible destination understand the dynamic weather patterns Juneau is subjected to. Juneau's location in Southeast Alaska designates it as a lush rainforest and rainforests are accompanied by weather that can change in a heartbeat. It's very possible to begin a morning in Juneau with a clear and sunny sky only to need a heavy rain jacket and boots within moments. Unique wind patterns and the elevation of mountains in this area mean that while the weather seems clear downtown, near and around the Mendenhall glacier, waters could be dangerously choppy. Many visitors to Juneau are dismayed when on a clear blue-sky day their tour company suddenly cancels excursions to glaciers by kayak. Ultimately, this is a safety move on the part of tour companies who understand high winds around the glacier could be disastrous for travelers observing by kayaks or canoes susceptible to flipping in harsh waves.

Similarly, tour companies hosting glacier hikes may only have limited spots available to visitors with good reason. While the glacier and mountain landscape that makes up this city is stunning, it's also changing at a rapid pace. In order to preserve the integrity of receding glaciers, the city of Juneau continues to grant fewer annual permits for hiking the glacier in hopes of keeping it a viable natural wonder and tourist destination for years to come.

Remain Flexible

Just as Juneau promises to bring a variety of thrilling views, exceptional entertainment, and opportunities for exploration, it's worth your time to arrive in this capital city with your own promise of flexibility. The weather may change and wildlife may come and go but it's the anticipation of the unknown that makes this city so unique and those who come to Juneau with a mindset to match often find it to be a place that captures and holds a special place in their hearts long after they've left. Whether you find yourself here to relax and unwind, or have come to see just what you're capable of in the great outdoors, Juneau is a city that also promises not to disappoint.

About the Expert

Caitlyn Knuth is a lifelong writer who was inspired to put a pen to paper as a child long before spelling skills were acquired. Constantly captivated by the pictures words have the power to paint and the owner of a spirit that is always ready for the next travel adventure, she's found her muse alive and well through the process of exploring new cities and sharing what she's found with the world.

An initial trip to Juneau several years ago left a bigger impression than she originally expected. Prepared for bears, she fell in love at first sight with the whales that call this area home. Unaccustomed to the raincoat culture that is essential to Juneau, she found herself enamored with the endless mist and fog that frequently roll in and give this rainforest packed city an enchanting take on weather patterns. It's a place that's hard to shake long after the trip has ended. When new cities follow you around, they're worth writing about. A passion for discovering the unexpected inspired her to put together a comprehensive guide to visiting the best of Juneau—with the understanding that this book is nothing more than an encouraging starting point to a greater adventure.

HowExpert publishes quick 'how to' guides on unique topics by everyday experts. Visit HowExpert.com to learn more.

Recommended Resources

www.HowExpert.com – Quick 'How To' Guides on Unique Topics by Everyday Experts.

www.HowExpert.com/writers- Write About Your #1 Passion/Knowledge/Experience.

www.HowExpert.com/membership - Learn a New 'How To' Topic About Practically Everything Every Week.

www.HowExpert.com/jobs - Check Out HowExpert Jobs.

Made in the USA
Monee, IL
15 December 2020